Openness and Visibility a memoir

*An history of hope, healing
and embracing a new life*

Mayan Goodwill

Ordering Information:

Prime Seven Media
518 Landmann St.
Tomah City, WI 54660

Printed in the United States of America

Openness …

"I do not believe that sheer suffering teaches. If suffering alone taught, all the world would be wise, since everyone suffers. To suffering must be added mourning, understanding, patience, love, openness and the willingness to remain vulnerable".

Anne Morrow Lindbergh.

Visibility…

"The power of visibility can never be underestimated".

Margaret Cho

This memoir is dedicated to my grandmother,
Transito Gonzalez, my family, and grandchildren.

I like to be thanked, my publisher and editor, Mr/Mrs for their feedback and input to writing this book, I have learned a lot about creative writing and linking my thoughts and memories to summarise each chapter of my past traumas, grief and lived experiences as survivor of a broken family, of civil war in El Salvador. I become a husband, father and grandfather, and an experienced therapist and as a migrant in Australia. My love and appreciation to my family for their emotional support and encouragement to write about me and my past. To my three grandchildren, I adore, Alfie, Artie and baby Maeve for their cuddles and special moments their shared with me, when they come over and spent quality time together with us- on video calls, face to face to have a laugh and connect each block of Lego toys, to complete each set, and enjoyed what we created with them. And finally, my grandmother, Transito, for being the person who cared and raised me and influenced the person that I am today.

"Fear is a natural response[1-2] to traumatic situations. Post-traumatic stress disorder (PTSD) develops in some people who have experienced a shocking, scary, or dangerous event. PTSD symptoms may include flashbacks, nightmares, severe anxiety, and uncontrollable thoughts about the event[3]".

TABLE OF
CONTENTS

INTRODUCTION

I have written this book to share with you, the reader, my personal account and history, prior to my migration to Australia. I have had thought about writing this memoir for many years, and it is long overdue project for me. I aways wanted to write about my life and I journey as migrant to Australia. This book is about a history of stages of my life; a child, a young man and a adult men, who never had a "normal" childhood nor youth, as my life's circumstances makes up me grow up out of the reality of my family and society where I grow up in. I was born in a third world country, where families values and social systems were broken by family domestic violence and civil war. I lived in an unpredictable and unsafe environment where you are essentially surviving each day in society. I have made choices to keep myself safe and alive. This memoir covers chapters of stages of my life including, when I experienced child traumas, when I had moments of grief, when the first time I witness before my eyes, social injustice, when I have flashback moments due to being triggered of present experiences, my long journey of healing, growth, hope and flourishing in life.

A glance on those pivot moments prior to writing this book

I am a survivor of torture and trauma, and I was diagnosed with PTSD in my early 30s. Fear has been an emotion and reaction for me for many years, mostly, when I have felt unsafe, and without a sense of belonging and disconnected with those people I loved or to whom I work with. / This fear dictated my life's choices for many years, it become part of me, after some many traumatic experiences I had as I growth up. I thought, I could never overcome this emotion and reaction- I was on a stage of survival all the time, and I thought, the best solution was to fleet my motherland and migrate to another country. It was difficult to live a "normal life" when you have a constant emotion and reaction of fear controlling your life. For me, fear was very physical, I felt a cold chill sensation in the back of my spine, all the way down to my feet and then my energy levels would deplete. This emotion and reaction of fear was the impact of lived experiences I have had, including, Family Domestic Violence and State Violence due to civil war during the 80s thru the 90s in El Salvador. These two factors impacted on me, psychologically, emotionally and physically.

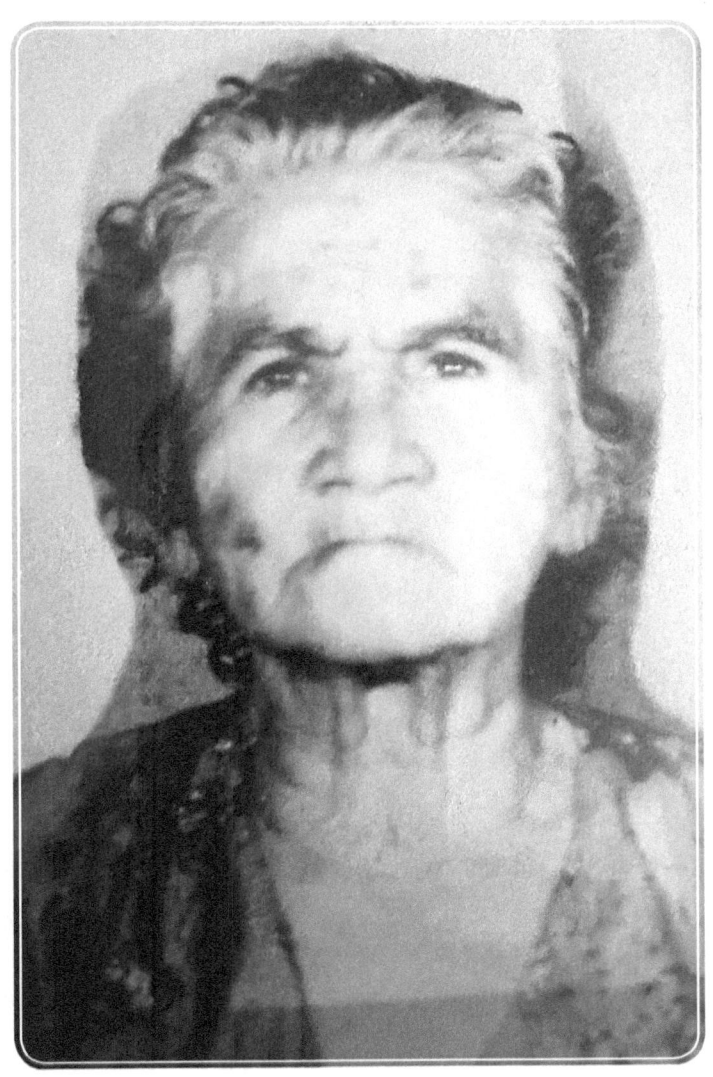

Transitó Gonzalez

CHAPTER ONE

Glimpse of childhood and youth memories.

*I*t was Saturday, a sunny day of spring/summer over the weekend, while I was sat down on my kayak, holding a paddle, floating over the calm waters of the Barley Griffith Lake, when memories of my grandmother, my childhood and teenage years, of my life back in El Salvador, came to my mind. As I sat on my kayak, I realised how blessed I was, to be raised by my grandmother, Trancito, she was the person, who I trusted, she was my hero. She took me in, when I was a newly born baby, as my mother felt she was too young to care of me. She taught me to be a good person, the importance of study and work, provide for yourself, and values of fairness, justice and to helping others in need. She was my mother, father, and role model. I remembered her persona, she was a tall person in her 80s, Caucasian, with golden locks, short hair and with smile in her face each time she saw me. She taught me to be independent and to take care of myself. When I started primary school, she prepared my lunch box and backpack, each morning for school, with a bottle of water. In the mornings, she used to walk with me to school, at the beginning of my first and second years of school and gradually, she

1

left me walked by myself when I felt more confident. Before I started my first year at school, I missed my first year, as my father did not registered me on time for my birth certificate. My grandmother was very upset with him, as apparently, he registered me in a different register jurisdiction where I was born, with the wrong birth date, and because of this, I started schooling a year later. I was disappointed as all my friends started that year their first year of school, and I ended up staying home. The following year, I remembered how excited I was to finally start school, as I wanted to wear my brand-new school uniform, shining shoes and my backpack. I do not recall if a photo of me with my wearing my uniform with my class and teacher was taken that day, but what I remembered was my grandmother walked me to school that day, as we walked, she hold my hand till we got to school. Schooling in El Salvador is only half a day to allow other students to study in the afternoon due to not having enough schools in the city.

After school, I walked home by myself, as it was only about 3 blocks away, from my grandmother's and I home. There were times, when I walked to school in the morning that I could heard gun shots in the distance, or other times police's car alarms. Also, I remembered that while I walked on walk paths, or crossing the streets, I would come across, human's parts laid on the side path walks. Sometimes, I would see fingers, or hands, or human heads, even human torsos without limbs. I was just a 8 years old, child at that time, and I was already exposed to witnessed how humanity was loss in our El Salvadorean society, where dignity and respect for human life seemed not to exist. I used to heard our neighbours, would spoke with my grandmother about "the conflict"; civil war in our country. I just could not understand the meaning nor the connection of finding human part on the way to school at that time with the civil war. Now, that I reflecting on what I was exposed as a child, I would considered that I did loss my innocent as a child for what I saw back then, but I was not sure, as finding human part was during the 80s and 90s in the streets was "normal". My grandmother used to advise me, if I saw any human parts, not to touch them, nor pick them up. I always respected my grandmother's advise, and I never did touch them as I felt afraid. But I remembered the strong smell coming off the bodies parts, as a child I learned the smell of death. To protect myself I used to cover my mouth and nose with my right hand, for no letting the smell of death get into my nose. Then, suddenly, I managed to get back to my present moment, sat down on my kayak, floating over the calm water, holding with my two hands the puddle in that sunny day, I could feel a gently sudden breeze, in my face and needed to adjust my helmet and to be able to see where I was going. The breeze continues and I could see the branches of the willows' threes, touching gently the water on the lake, it was like a gentle dance on the tip of the branches, floating over the water. Then, I decided that It was time to get back home. I reach the water edge and stoop up and got out the kayak and packed everything in my Ute. As I stood up, I stand still for a moment and I breathed in and out gently a few times and said to myself, "*I am grateful for the gift of life*". It started to get late, and I drove back home that afternoon, to be with my family that I love so much.

The day I met my estranged biological father.

One day, while visiting the National Arboretum Canberra— a place of legacy of variety of threes forest for future generations, my family and I were seated waiting for our lunch order, then memories come back to me, this time, I remembered when I turned 13, I was riding my bike that afternoon near my home, when I saw two men, they were walking towards our house, they stopped once they came near our home, one of the men looked familiar to me, but I far as I knew, I never met him before, he walked towards me and he was about to say something, but then, my grandmother, stopped him and asked, "what are you doing here?". Apparently, she knew the man. I could see that he was drunk, as his speech was not clear, he was mumbling. He then, responded to my grandmother's question, "I am here to see my son", he replied," *my son?"* I asked myself. Since my grandmother took me under her care, the only time she mentioned my father was when he makes a mess of my school first year enrolment, but never again, so did my mother, she never spoke about my father till one day she disclosed to me, that they have me out of love but she declined his offer to move in with him as she was not ready for a relationship. My mother was a teenager at that time. I asked my mother if my father asked for me after they separated, she replied *"he never forgives me for to not wanting to be with him and he decided to walk away from her and me since"*. This stuck with me for long time, as a teenager myself, but I always was proud of my mother's honesty and forthcoming to share with me, the circumstances on how I come to this world. After my mother's told me her reason for not wanting to be with my father, I respected her more and understood her. On the other hand, I could not understand, my father's neglectful and indifference behaviour as father and not able to respect my mother's choice which shown lack of respect for women. This was something uncomfortable for me, for long time as a male, as never wanted to be like my father, unresponsible and disrespectful to the mother of her child. I want to be a better person and a man with principles and good values of dignity of respect to others, particularly, women, as my grandmother, taught me.

After, I heard what the man, who apparently alleged to be my estranged biological father, I told to my grandmother, that I was shocked, as I never expected to ever meet my father, I had ever seen him not even in a photograph till that day. Every time, I wanted to know about my father, my grandmother and mother always were reluctant to talk about him. The man, who claimed to be father, then he told me *"If you become one of them-communists...I'll kill you"*. I was not sure what he meant with his words, but I understood his treat. Then, I saw my grandmother gotten upset for what the man said to me, and she told him *"I just cannot believe that you just come here to treating your son, aren't you?"* He, then walked away with his friend and disappeared in the distance, as he always has, I could no process what just happened. A man out of the blue, visited us just to threaten me, but why I was puzzled by it. My grandmother said that she heard that my father was in the military, and he had changed since, he become arrogant and have superiority problems. She comforted me and asked if I was ok, I replied *"yes, I am ok grandmom"*. Later that day, questions started inside of my ahead, why he never asked about my schooling, how I was doing, nor if he was happy to see me. I had never had any male role models in my life. Earlie that day, when I saw my biological father for the first time as he walked toward my home and told me what he told me, that was the first and last time I ever saw him. I never understood why my father was so angry and treated me, as he never helped me on anything not even my schooling. My mother said to me not to waste my time to find him as he was a bad man. And I never did. But now after many decades later, I still wondered, when my father decided to visited my grandmother and I, that if he was not drunk and genuine wanted to meet me, his son, to rebuild a father son relationship, how different would have been, as I always wanted to know if I have siblings on his side of his family, a grandmother aunties or uncles. But I guess I would never know.

My grandmother and my mother told me a few months later, of the brief visit of my father, that they found out that he was in the military and no wonder why he behaved and threatened me in the way he did. Prior to the unexpected visit of my father, I remembered that my grandmother told me that having a family member in the military back on her days, was an honourable thing to have then, but since the civil war started, she said. She continued said that *"They are taught to hate people even their own family"*. I found sad and heartbreaking that a person would accept and be convinced to harm and kill even his own family for the interest of government. I could not comprehend back then why so much hate from my father towards me and he only wanted to see me when he was drunk. I felt disappointed for a while but I my grandmother will cheer me up. After many years, after met my father, even thought it was hurtful, I realised that perhaps he, was part of an abusive, controlling and oppressive system designed to spread fear in society by maintaining a culture of death. As I wrote these words I got sweat and cold feet. I may have been triggered to share this with you the reader, but not to worry I am practising my mindfulness and breathing exercises as I continued writing, to self-regulate and continue with my day. Suddenly One of my family asked, "hello where are you". And then, I returned to the present moment, we were sat down, leaning our arms into the table waiting for our lunch order in the indoor cafe area at the Arboretum. It was a quiet weekend that afternoon. As we still waiting for our lunch, I could see the outdoor surroundings thru the big and wide glass windows The glass windows were fitted into the main building all the way from the ceiling to the floors and the design, gave all people who visited the arboretum, a stunning view of the black mountain with the Telstra Tower over the horizon and part of the Barley Griffing lake. We enjoyed our lunch and a couple hours later we drove off back home.

The picnic group on Sunday.

Another relaxing weekend at home sat down in my chair and feeling the warm of a fireplace in our backyard this afternoon. Is midday and the sun is up but still a bit chilly outside. I am holding a nice cupper of coffee while my family is preparing a glaze platter in the kitchen. Then memories of past come back to me, this time, was when I am still 13-year-old. On Sunday mornings a group of two nuns, from the local church used to come over to our community and invited all teenagers under 15, if they were interested to join them for a prayer picnic, the place where they used take the teenagers was across the other side of bridge to where we lived, my friends and I used to call "the houses of the rich people". The houses were mansion, almost a block size, the front yard had nicely mowed green grass with threes. The nuns liked the houses as it was a quiet, clean and safe area, for the group of teenagers to have light lunch and prayers. I went about 3 times with the teenagers' group and the two nuns for prayer's picnics; they were kind and generous by given us free lunch on Sunday. But, one day, after prayers and we were about to walked back home, I asked the nuns, a question that I have been wanting to ask them for a while, and finally, I felt confident to do so, and then I asked them *"why the houses and gardens here are so big and nice, compare to where we lived in our humble but poor community"*. The nun responded by saying that *"it is God's will that some people are rich and others poor, but when you died and go to heaven, you will have everything you want if you follow his commandments"*. I was not happy with her response, and I said to her that *"it was not God's will, but men that has created these differences for some people to be rich and other poor, and why we need to wait till we died and go to heaven when we can have a good life in earth"*. The nun was unhappy with me and the way I thought. After that Sunday, they never invited me to their picnics. I told my grandmother, and she asked the nuns the follow Sunday when they come over to our community and they said to her that I have a black mind, and I was a not good influence to other teenagers in the study group. My grandmother stood up for me and she said to them *"no he does not have black mind, he's a good boy"*.

But the nuns refused to invite me to their group picnic from that day on. I felt that the nuns did not like being challenged their way of thinking, but I just could not accept their simplistic view of reality and inequality I saw before my eyes. My family comes with a nice glaze platter, and we enjoyed each other company that afternoon.

At nigh more memories come to me on more time, this time when I finished school, year 10, but I just could not continue schooling, as I needed to start learning a trade to help my grandmother and myself. The first job I did was, spray painting and panel beating, I tried for a few months, but the fumes of the paint were very chemical for me. Later, I tried bricklaying with my stepfather, but it was not what I wanted to do as a trade, but I went with the flow anyway as I needed income. I always wanted to continue studying and complete year 12 and then applied for university to learn about society, history, politics and the economy, but in El Salvador such opportunities are only for young people with rich parents. The opportunities for me to study university was just that a dream. I eventually, gave up my dream, and I settled to working as brick laying labour. These skills helped me even today to do handyman jobs at home as I understand the basics of building. I finally felt tired and decided to wind down, so I headed to bed that night.

CHAPTER TWO

My four cousins

I sat down in my couch tonight, in the living room in my house, in front of me there is a bookcase, where I can see my favourites books; on of them The New Earth by Eckart Tolle. As I contemplate the bookcase with my books, I remembered my cousins that I grew up with back when I lived in El Salvador.

Most of my male cousins were killed during the civil war, their history of loss generation that make me sad to tell but I feel compel to share their individuals' histories as I am one of the three survivors of my generation with my two other male cousins that we make it through, and they live in El Salvador. They never did anything wrong, nor were involved in politics, but rather they were victims by the hands of the military in El Salvador during the 80s. They were four male cousins that their deaths were unjustified, but I want to write their histories to keep their memories and histories alive and never to fade away.

One of them was my cousin, Roberto, he was 25 years old married man, who loved his family, and father of three children and worked to support his family. I remembered him as someone who was kind and loyal to his family and lived near by my grandmother and me. The day he died, I remembered hearing guns shoots fired closed to our community, rumours in the community spread that students and soldiers were in confrontation during a students' demonstration protesting against the government for cuts to the science institute located near by our community. People's rumours included that some students were killed during the crossfire between students and soldiers in front of the Institute that afternoon. For some unknown reason, I felt a strong need to go to the institute to see what has happened. After I waited for the guns shoots to stopped, I decided to walked to the institute and check if there was someone who may needed help to call ambulance to get them medical and hospital care as they needed. I walked and took me about 7 minutes to get to the Institute, on my arrival I saw only one person lay down on the main entrance of the Institute, I walked closer to the body and I was shocked when I recognised him, it was my cousin Roberto death lying down on his back and half of his face was complete imploded by guns shoot in a pool of blood. It was so sad to saw him lifeless and being killed in the way he died. I asked other onlookers to get a blanket or something to cover his face with and one of them gave a brown towel and I covered my cousin's face with it. An ambulance arrived right after I placed the brown towel on his face, I told the ambos that he was my cousin for ID his body and then they took him to the public morgue that afternoon. I never told my grandmother what I saw that day as did not want her to worry. No counselling nor welfare check on me as days and weeks passed by, as there is not such mental health support in our country, they did not exist during the 80s. I managed in the best way I could, I remembered had nightmares some nights and feeling sick and no appetitive. Time passed by and my cousin's death seen to become a memory and an history that our family were not comfortable to talk about as no one wanting to become suspicious of his death was associated with students protecting against the government. A few later, a witnessed confined on me what he saw and what happened to my cousin. The witness told me that him and my cousin went to the institute as he was told that one of his daughters was at the Institute and for this reason he was there with my cousin. Both went to look for my cousin's daughter but she was no there and he decided to get out of the institute through the back exit but my cousin went to the front entrance instead and as he walked to the exit the institute through the front gate a military vehicle with heavy shoot gun and soldiers started shooting and unfortunately my cousin was the only person walking out the institute through the main gate and he was instantly killed. He had a dignified funeral and there was never a investigation nor justice for his death.

My second cousin was, Mauricio, a twin who was in his 20s the night of his death there was national curfew in San Salvador. My auntie told me his sad history, as I was not present on what happened to him. My auntie said that earlier that day he was killed by the military, he just found out that his girlfriend was pregnant of their first baby and he celebrated with friends at her home through the evening and he got drunk and without thinking he decided to walked out the house and went to the main road, yelling and screaming how happy he was to become a father. My auntie and two of his friends tried to took him back home, but he didn't listen and then they decided to go back to my auntie's house and get some sheets to wrapped him and bring him home. As all went back home and started to get the sheets to get my cousin back home, they heard guns shoots up the road and then screams, then they realised that if they went to assist my cousin they also could be killed and waiting all night till earlier in the morning to go and check on my cousin Mauricio. When they went to check on Mauricio, they found him death by gun shoots and left bled till he died. My auntie was in tears telling me the history of my cousin, father to be, who was killed for celebrating his girlfriend pregnancy of their first child. No investigation nor justice for my cousin's death. His girlfriend left my auntie's home after my cousin's funeral as it was to painful her and could not continue living with my aunties after.

My third cousin was Julio, he was a 25-year-old single man who just started his own mechanic business when he was killed. He loved fixing motor cars and be his own boss. My cousin and I were very close as we grow up together. Our families used to take us to trips to local rivers for swimming and we played football on the weekends with friend after Sunday's mass. I felt sad in my heart and grief his death for long time. My mother was told his history by my auntie, when she visited her in San Salvador. My mother lives in New York with my two sister and 9 nephews and she likes to visit family back in El Salvador. My mother told me my cousin's history of what happened to him. My auntie told my mother that my cousin the day he was killed, he was working in his business, and he decided to go for lunch to near pupusaria restaurant. As he was leaving the restaurant to back to work, he was caught between crossfire between soldiers and anti-government protesters. He was gunned in the crossfire, and he was killed for not reason. My auntie still asking for an investigation for my cousin's death but her demands for justice go into deaf ears.

My four cousin his name was Marcos; he was bother of my cousin Julio. He was his youngest younger brother; they have two sister who were married and have three nephews. Marcos never married and didn't have children. He was a quite and private person who worked with my cousin, Julio in his mechanic business. My auntie told my mother, when she visited her while on holidays in San Salvador, that my cousin was killed in crossfire when soldiers were apparently shooting at young men who were allegedly against the government in one of the colleagues in San Salvador. Similar to Julio and Roberto, Marcos seemed to be at the wrong place at the wrong time, but I believed that discriminatory shooting by soldiers played a significant part of my cousin's death. Compared to Australia, laws have changed for the safety of alleged suspicious driver to no pursue them by police's cars to reduce risk and harm to such suspected and the public. In El Salvador, many, especially young people were killed in discriminated shooting by authorities without consequences of their actions and with impunity.

I feel sad for the loss of my cousin for their death and leaving so soon. Telling their histories is not easy, as I do get triggered of my own trauma and grief, but I do believe that their lives and memories deserve to be known land acknowledged, to keep their memories alive and do not let them disappear as time goes on. They memories will always live in me, and when you the reader, read this memoir contributes to pay respect and care.

CHAPTER THREE

Turning 18

*I*t was a long weekend holidays when we decided to spend quality family time together with my daughter, and our two grandchildren in a caravan park. This caravan park is like our second home for us, we have been staying at park for the last 15 years. We had visited others parks in the area, but they are not the same, as we feel connected and at our second home, each time we stayed in Merry Beach. After we set up our new Jayco caravan, we sat in our chairs and started enjoying our surroundings, the ocean breeze and the sea view from our camping site. As the day went by, I felt sleep and dreamed that night when I turned 18. During this period in my life, I become an adult and with the support of my mother and grandmother I managed to completed year 8 of my secondary schooling. I felt accomplished but I knew that I need to continue studying and I always wanted to study university level. But life sometimes does not go as you hope to be. During this time, I have the most painful experience, that I was not prepared for, my grandmother who raised me, died.

One day she decided to visit one of my aunties and she said to me, "I *will be back home later*". I replied ok Abuelita *"tenga cuidado nos vemos pronto"* ok be careful, see you soon. I stayed home, as my new girlfriend was with me that day. It started to get late, and I noticed that my grandmother still has not come home, I started to be worried and waited and waited. My girlfriend and I decided to have dinner by ourselves and left some food, for my grandmother, when she returns home. We went to bed and felt asleep. I remembered that night nothing seemed to be alright, then, I woke up as I could heard my girlfriend crying next to me and I asked her *"what's was wrong"* and she respond, *" I saw your grandmother ghost, sat on the edge of the bed rubbing your head with her hand and she asked to promised her that I will look after you"* and then she disappeared. I comforted her and suggested her to get back to sleep. That nigh I had nightmares of cars coming from everywhere and runed over me.

The next day, we released that my grandmother did came back and then we decided that my girlfriend left for work, and I went to my auntie's home as I wanted to know if my grandmother stayed over at her place the night before. I knotted my auntie's house door, and she opened it and asked her *"if my grandmother come over yesterday for a visit"* and she responded, *"no she did not come home last night"*, Then, I asked my auntie if she could help me to look for her and she agreed, we went to my other auntie's house and the said the same, that my grandmother has not visited her neither. Then, my aunties and I decided to start calling hospitals, to check with them, if my grandmother was admitted last night, but the hospital staff said that *"not she was not on their records for admission last night"*. I started to feel anxious and more worry. Then, we decided to go to the public morgue, the public morgue is a place when council workers collect human remains found overnight on the public streets to be identified by family members. The public morgue is a confronting place and scene, as they open the gates of a big freezer for the public to see the human bodies or remains inside of it. We could see a few complete human bodies from where were standing, we can see the body of a young women with jeans but her upper bode naked, also a young men's body but not sight of my grandmother's body in the public morgue.

Several days past by and about 10 days later, one of my aunties received a call from the hospital. They said that they collected a women's body about 10 days ago and they keep her in the morgue but because no one come forward to identify her, they decided to buried her into a mass grave. The news felt like a stub into my heart, and I was inconsolable for days. My mother later was giving the news of what happened to me grandmother and she asked to the hospital is a was possible to exhumed her remains, but they said it was not allow due to issues of health and safety for council workers if they exhumed human remains, after having days of being buried with other bodies. As we were in shocked and grief we forgot to ask the hospital the circumstances of my grandmother's death. 3 days later, my auntie asked the hospital staff, the location of where they found my grandmother's body. They gave to my auntie the location and we went together to where my grandmother was the last place she was found death and her body collected to the public morgue. For our surprised, the location where the accident happened, it was near our community, on the side of the road next to the east bus interchanged. She appeared to be had run over by a large vehicle due to her injuries and fractures.

The next day, I went with my mother and two aunties to the location, where the hospital staff told us, that they took possession of my grandmother's body. As we walked and look around the streets, we saw a car dealership across the road. We decided to go, and we went in into the reception office and asked staff if they could help us if they remembered seen a car accident and a pedestrian being run over and died, a few weeks ago. Then, two staff members come forward and confirmed that they saw the accident and the pedestrian that died. One of them told us that, the pedestrian was waiting in the middle of the road to cross the street, when a jeep vehicle, hit the pedestrian and did not slow down to aid the injured pedestrian. The other one staff member said that he had written the number plate of the jeep and gave it to us. We described my grandmother, and the car dealer staff confirmed that the pedestrian was my grandmother. They confirmed with us that they would be happy to be witness of the accident if we decide to open a case to the court to investigate and found the people who killed my grandmother.

The next day, my mother and aunties contacted the magistrate court and applied to open the case for the dead of my grandmother, the investigate and bring those responsible for her death of my grandmother into justice. We all waited, patiently, and finally, two months later, we received a letter from the magistrate invited us to attend to the hearing of the case of the dead of my grandmother.

The day of reckoning

The court hearing was held at the local magistrate court, we arrived early at the court that morning, as we hoped to see those responsible for the death of my grandmother. A hour later, the two staff of the car leadership arrived and we started talking amongst ourselves about the case, and hopeful we were that justice system can help us to bring those responsible for the death of my dear grandmother. As we waited, minutes felt like weeks and then 30 minutes later, three army officers arrived and walked straight into the court, where the hearing for the case was about to start. The army officers were wearing sunnies with their officer's cups and wearing their formal officer's uniform with their shining shoes. They were stoic with no facial expression, they never looked at us, they completed ignored us, and they walked straight into the court hearing and sat down at their allocated seats.

Then, something we never expected, happened. After the two witnesses saw the three officers, they seemed afraid, I saw fear in their faces, the court hearing was about to start when, they approached us and told us with their whispering voices that, they had changed their minds, and they could not go into the court room as witness. They further said to my mother that, they did not expect that the people who killed your mother were Army's Offices. Then, they left the magistrate right after they told my mother how they felt. They left us with shocked and disbelieved. The clerk told us that the hearing was about to start, we walked into the court room, and we sat on the side area where the magistrate desk was to our left and the three offers sat in front of the magistrate. I heard the clerk exclaimed" all stand up, the magistrate is entering the room". The court processing started, and we thought, perhaps the case can continue without the two witnesses. But I was wrong, the magistrate come out and sat in front of the three-army officer in their uniforms with sunnies and hats on and then he said, "The hearing for the case has been withdrawn as there is no evidence, nor witnesses of wrongdoing". Then, clerk requested, to stood up as the magistrate walked of the court hearing. I remembered the magistrate, stood and he walked out the hearing room, he kept his head down as he out. I was confused and full of rage as he never had eye contact with us nor asked us any questions during his brief time as magistrate to fulfil his role. I also, I wondered myself, why he never asked any questions to the army officers, nor had eyes contact with the officers. I thought, does the army has more power than the legal system in our country? It was a day reckoning for me that day.

I had something like out of body experienced, not like a having dream but waking up in the middle of the night with a nightmare. I always was puzzled, by the same question over and over inside of head; like our two witnesses, was also, the magistrate afraid of the army officers? I never had the answered.

After what we just witnessed what happened, at the court hearing, right in front of eyes, we felt angry with a strong sense of injustice and dissolution of the El Salvador's legal system. But inside of my heart I could feel a sense of warm and determination, and I said to myself, I won't let the system broke me. I saw the three men walked past in front of me and my family, out the court room, with a smile in their faces. They did not spoke a word since their arrival, nor eye contact with us. The killers of grandmother walked out the court hearing with impunity, arrogance and complete disregard of their criminal actions, they walked and went into their military vehicles and drove away that day from the magistrate, like nothing has happened. That day was our very first day that we experienced as family, with the legal system in our country. My mother, aunties and I, were left, feeling defeated and powerless and let down by our legal system, that supposed to protect people from injustices.

Before our first encounter with the El Salvador's legal system, we were ordinary good citizens, that never had any issues as we always respected the law, we were humble working-class people, that provided for ourselves, we never depended on any government assistance nor welfare in our country. My mother was a business owner, she had a fruit and coffee shop, and I worked in construction in casual basis. We thought that our good standing citizens status could be considered during the court hearing for the case to investigate and charge those responsible for the death of my grandmother, but it did not matter. We also, notice that there was not empathy on behalf of the magistrate during the hearing, to our loss in our family, this was unacceptable and complete disregarded by the magistrate to fulfill his role to representing the law and be impartial. That day I felt, I was living in a nightmare, I asked myself, how people working in the legal system can be so corrupted, cold hearted, negligent, and have complete disregard and disrespectful of other peoples' lives with impunity.

My mother and aunties went to their homes that day. I met my girlfriend in a park near the courts. I told her that I felt deflated and betrayed by the legal system for what I just experienced. She hugged me tight and gave a kiss on my chicks, and did not say anything, as she knew, what I needed. In my heart I just could not accept that my grandmother, the person who raised me, I could not give her a dignified funeral, she deserved, not a tomb, where I can take flowers and prayed. I was not able to say, thank you for raising me, and goodbye. Weeks, months and years went by and my grief for the loss of my grandmother and the injustice no to bring those responsible for her death, never heal. I felt for many years that my heart physically hurt. It was like a cut deep in my heart. I got triggered, overtime I saw any person wearing a military uniform. I remembered, my heart going faster, and I had shallow breathing, like running but stand still; more like internal powerless feeling and unable to self-regulate, like my heart is going to come out of mouth feeling.

In El Salvador back in the 80s and 90s, mental health services were non-existence for the average citizen, to help you process and healing your grief, trauma or anxiety issues. You lived in a society that if you are a suspected communist, then you would be persecuted, tortured, gone missing or killed. You were afraid of your own government and the military, as they had control and power over its citizens. My experiences that I had with the impunity of the death of my grandmother, demonstrated to me that I can decided to do good and be part of humanity by helping other in needs as my grandmother taught me. I missed her so much, her smile, her persona and aura around her that make felt at easy and peace of mind.

My grandmother was a character, she was direct and very assertive person who spoke her mind. Her love, care and patience to me were a God gifts. Growing up with her has shaped the person I am today. Her guidance and mentoring to think about helping others have been the foundation of my core values: to see the potential in each person that come across on my path of my life. My daughter asked," *hey Dad, wake up is dinner time*" I felt embarrassed, then I replied "*yes, I'll start cooking then*". This time, it was my daughter who brought me back to the present moment. The sunset was beautiful that evening with clouds changing colours from red to orange and a gently cool ocean breeze. I finished BBQ meat, and we all sat down and eat at the table and as I saw my daughter, son in-law and two grandchildren I told myself. Life's an interesting and wonderful journey and we enjoyed each other's company that evening in our second Merry Beach.

CHAPTER FOUR

Altruism and generosity

The day that my grandmother died, I felt a sense of emptiness and took me a long time to recover, I was loss for a while with no direction nor purpose. My mother told me one day that there was a new housing program to help people in my situation. I went to the place that the coordinator planned to meet and greet people willing to sign on an agreement with the local council to own a 10 square meters block of land and low monthly repayments. I saw the land and its location, and the council staff asked us to go and choose the block I wanted. I walked up the hill in front of me, and then I reached the top, I saw a big lake in the distance bellow the ground level as a volcano crater that it has been filled with water. It was the Ilopango. It was a stanning view, I though this the block I want to build y own home, then I told the council workers that I was happy to take the block where I was standing. I signed the documents, and I felt excited for the first time, after being grieving the passing of my grandmother. I went to visit my mother later that day, and I told her the news, she was very happy for me.

New home new beginnings

I started building a small house by myself after I was given all building materials I needed, by the council. It took me about a week to complete my new home in my own block of land with overview of the Ilopango Lake. There were more people doing the same. I offered them help with building their homes of flatten the block of land, and I they accepted my offer to help them. After a few months things started to go downhill. I felt depressed and lonely. I could not understand why I felt that way as I had my own house and block of land. But I remembered that neither my mother nor my sister never visits me, and this did not help. I started to recent my mother and I realised that perhaps she wanted to get rid of me by supporting me to live away from the city. I tried to be positive as much as I could, even, I volunteer to the youth group in the community. We organised a social event with music and food, and we were able to collect some funds, but still, this was not enough for me. I decided to visit my mother and confronted her, about why she wanted me to take the block of land and she told that her intentions were never about me to live far away from her, but for me to own, my own block of land and to own my house. I never got alone with stepfather partner as he was someone without any empathy for anyone. After a few months, I reluctantly decided to give back the block of land as my mental health gotten worse.

I moved in with friends back in the city, I wanted to focus on finding work. My flatmates invited me to visit where they worked as volunteers in a NGOs and they got food humpers and free medical care. Little I would know that there, I meet the future mother of my children. She was completing a First Aid course at the NGOs centre, and she use to smile each time I saw her. We started being friends and we become very close. I was given the opportunity to work as volunteer is a community development program to support displaced peasant families coming to the city away from indiscriminatory bombings in their house and land by the Salvadorian army. I felt positive and with a sense of purpose to know that I could help others in need. I have the humble privilege to met and worked with Drs. We had Doctors from Doctors without Borders helping us to learn about immunisation for children, women and adults. I would say that finally, I found a place and a group of people who were altruistic and humanistic in nature to helping others, and I felt that I found meaning and purpose back into my life

Altruistic work in NGOs

I found myself becoming a volunteer member of a NGO's helping internal refugees migrating from rural communities to the city of San Salvador escaping indiscriminatory bombings to their houses and land by the Salvadorian military. These refuges were mostly families, hungry, heartbroken, homeless, unemployed with little knowledge on how live in a city, as the majority were peasants living out of their land sustainable living. The NGOs received international Aid Funds donations from abroad, we had volunteer Doctors from Doctors Without Borders who trained us to vaccinate and provide First Aid and wound care for free for people living on marginalised communities. Two of the Doctors working with us where from Australia and they told me how life was in down under, but I never thought that their information may be helpful later in my life.

During my time working at the NGOs, I met the mother of my children. She was a teenager who came to the center to learn how to administer vaccines and provide First Aid. Over time, she began to catch my attention—she would smile and giggle whenever our eyes met. A natural chemistry developed between us, and we eventually became a couple. After a year together, we decided to get married in a civil ceremony at the local council office in Soyapango. We never had a honeymoon, as our focus at the time was on continuing our work—supporting families living in marginalized communities in San Salvador. We regularly visited these communities to vaccinate children (with parental consent), the elderly, and pregnant women to help prevent avoidable illnesses.

The Frontier

One day we were invited to a meeting organised by the NGOs Director. He stated that we needed to create a group of volunteers in our organisation to go the EL Salvador and Guatemala borders as donations from the US' NGOs has been stopped by the Salvadorian army for not valid reason. The group of volunteers was to help raise awareness in the media about Salvadorean army's unjustifiable blocked of donations into El Salvador to our NGOs communities in needs. The two trucks full on donations were stopped for about a week at that time. My family and I agreed to support the cause. Two days later, the NGOs organised a bus to get all volunteers to the border between Guatemala with El Salvador, to demonstrate against Salvadorean government that has stopped two semi-trailers to enter the country for our NGOs organisation. The two containers were full of donations by sisters NGOs in the US. The containers have a lot of clothing, shoes, wheelchairs, and medical and prosthetics equipment. The donations were needed to our give them out to the communities we helped at that time in San Salvador. Also to set up a community clinic in our centre to provide medical care for those who needed and those who could not afford to pay for Drs consultations and medications. We took the bus earlier in the morning and after 2 hours on the road we got to the border. There were a lot of soldiers in the border that were blocked the road on the side of EL Salvador, but the Guatemala side was open over the other side of the crossing bridge. We got the banner out and we started demanding that the donations must be allowed to enter the border. We stayed there for two days with not avail, the NGOs Director then decided that we need to get back to the city and call for a media conference to let Salvadorian know that was happing in the border.

A media conference was held the day after at the NGOs office in the city of San Salvador, and a few media organisation were invited to attend. I was supported by the Director to spoke on behalf of the NGOs and let Salvadorean community know that the two semi-trailers were stopped by the Salvadorian soldiers in the border for about a week without any substantial reason was inacceptable. Some media organisation asked me questions like *"We heard the donations are for guerrillas"*. I responded by saying, *"that was the excused by the Salvadorian soldiers to stopped the two semi-trailers to enter into the country", but it is not true, the donation were for our communities in needs as they had come to the city looking for safer place to live in the city"*.

After the media conference the two semi-trailers were finally allowed into the country. We all celebrated and felt happy and grateful for the decision of the Salvadorean government to allow the donations into the country. When the two semi-trailers arrived at the city, the Director for the NGOs was able to have a temporary storage big enough to store the donations. A few days later, we invited media organisation to witness, members of the NGOs hand out the donations to the communities. The NGOs where we worked were transparent, and prof wrong the Salvadorean government that the donations were for our communities in need. After the donations were received, The NGOs managed to setup community clinics run by members of the communities with Doctors of Doctor Without Border, that we were helping at that time. The community clinics were managed by community's leader to care for their communities' members by providing services including, medical check-ups, immunisation for children and pregnant women, and the elderly and first Aid for small injuries free of charge.

After the good work provided by the NGOs my family and I started to noticed that some work colleagues were nor attending work at the office in San Salvador. We become concerned as I found that one of our colleagues was arrested, and detained for three days for not reason, but I felt relief as she was released and told us her history. My work colleague who was released, told me that after the media conference, our NGOs was well known for the two trailer donations by the Salvadorean military, and she heard while detained that they will continue persecuting members of our NGOs. So, I leaned that all volunteer members of our NGOs started to be targeted by the Salvadorian soldiers and the Guardia National. Two weeks later, after my colleague was released, I noticed that two members went missing. The colleague that was arrested, she resigned as she did not felt safe to work in our organisation. My family and I started to feel afraid for our safety and our lives. For our misfortune, one day were in our way walking to our place when we saw an army platoon walking towards us and then we stopped walking they saw us and the leader of the military platoon asked to give him our backpacks and we cooperated and gave them our backpacks as we did not have anything to hide. The leader found pamphlets invitation to a meeting to our NGOs centre to collect donations, then he looked at us and the demanded to his soldiers to arrented us and they took us individual to the jeep military cars, and blindfolded us.

CHAPTER FIVE

State torture

This afternoon is a weekday, I was driving on my way back home, after work. As I drove, I started driving over the Scrivener Drive Dam bridge and I could see can see the Barley Griffing Lake to my right, driver's window, and then, as I passed the Dam, to my left, I drove passed the National Zoo & Aquarium' entrance, and, as I continue my journey, I could see the Telstra Tower in the distance, in front of me, but quickly disappeared behind the eucalyptus trees bushes, as I continue drove over the hill road of Lady Denman Road, then soon after, I started to drive down the road into the road suddenly there appeared front of me, signal lights, and then I turned to the left exit, just before the signal lights into Forrest Drive that if you continue can take can take you into the Arboretum, but I continued drove Forrest Drive that take you under the Tuggeranong Parkway Bridge when you turned right and then it convert into the Gungahlin Drive Extension (GDE) to drove home to north side of Canberra. I turned right to join the GDE and continue my journey to home. I arrived home 15 minutes later. I changed my work clothes and got myself cosy, sat down in the couch, and I got ready for the evening, then, I turned on the TV and I selected YouTube app, and I noticed that a new video of the favourites' channels; Nayid Bukele, the president elected for the second turn in El Salvador had a new video about his visit to Argentina. Then, I started to remembered the day and I was arrested.

While I was walking along a street near my home in San Salvador, a platoon of soldiers stopped me. The major asked for my backpack, and I handed it over. He seemed inexplicably angry, even though all he found inside were pamphlets from our NGO inviting people to a fundraiser. Despite this, he ordered his platoon to arrest me. They handcuffed and blindfolded us, and we were taken into individual military vehicles that afternoon. The major of the platoon decided to arrest us for no valid reason, I asked then why we were detained but they refused to answer me and took us to one of their vehicles, blindfolded us, and they drove us for a while. Then, they stopped, after they drove us for a while and they separated us took inside into a dark area, we knew it was the Guardia National barracks.as they walked me, I could hear it was a noisy place, when there were a lot of peoples' voices and screams everywhere. I felt terror

My illegal arrest took place just six months after my wedding. I was accused of being a 'Communist.' The barracks where I was taken had a notorious reputation—some detainees were tortured and later released, while others disappeared without a trace and were never found.

The Unit was called, "La Guardia National" an especial army of soldiers trained by US soldiers on Salvadorian's soil, and they were called "contra-communist forces". They had a notorious uniforms, helmets, weapons and military vehicles. When the Unit patrolled at night suburbs in San Salvador, they arrested any suspicious person that they thought it was too young to be in the stress. When people saw them in their vehicles, they will be scared and afraid and at times they hide from them. I remembered once, I was waiting for the bus to get home in Soyapango when they come in from nowhere and they saw with my backpack, they approached me and told to turn around, face the wall and open my legs. Then, on of the Guardia National soldiers told to open the legs more and took my backpack and he started looking through my personal items, but they didn't find anything that presented as reason to arrest me, also I think they didn't because there were a lot of people in the bus stop waiting for the bus, whom like me just wanted to get home that evening. They let me go and I felt a strong sense of relief but fear.

During the three nights I was illegally detained at the Guardia Nacional barracks, I was subjected to psychological torture. They kept me blindfolded and isolated. I could hear people screaming, sobbing, and pleading, 'please don't hurt me. I was threatened every two hours, and the soldiers wound asked me to whom I was working with and where my other co-workers were hiding. I was not able to sleep for the 3 nights, as constantly was woken up and they asked the same questions over and over. Each day, I pleaded with them to spare me from harm, but my requests were ignored. They continued to issue threats in an attempt to force answers from me. I remember the final night of my psychological torture while being illegally detained at the Guardia Nacional barracks. They told me that someone had 'confessed' on my behalf, claiming I was a communist and had been terrorizing people—things I had never done. Our crime was to be humanistic and socially conscious young couple to helping other Salvadorians in despaired that we saw their suffering, dispossession and displacement on their homes and communities and looking for a new start in their lives by seeking shelter to settle in into San Salvador, all caused by the indiscriminatory bombing in rural communities in El Salvador by the US backed Salvadoran army.

During the three days when the Guardia Nacional soldiers forcibly took me away, I was not allowed to see anyone else. This separation was used as a form of psychological torture. Those days felt like years for me, as I lost sense of time, taste, smell but my sense of hearing heighten, I could hear other's detainees' screams and sobbing with despair and fear for their lives, I realised, I was in torture chamber. I was so afraid that we may never see each other nor make it alive. On the last day, I was taken out of the cell, blindfolded, and for the first time, I heard a familiar voice nearby. It gave me hope that we might be released alive.

After the 3 days I was taken out the barracks and taken to the magistrate court by soldiers and they threatened me to say to the local clerk when asked who I pledge, to said "guilty" and they would let me go. So, as I wanted to be free, I agreed to say guilty. When we arrived to the magistrate, they took me to staff clerk and he asked me how I pledge and answered "guilty" then the soldiers laughed at me, and then the clerk asked one of the guard officers at the magistrate to cuffed me and take me inside to wait to be transported to a men's prison. Then, through the entrance, I saw another group of soldiers approaching the area where I was being held. For a moment, I felt a sense of relief, thinking the worst might be over. But I had no idea what was truly unfolding that day. Someone was taken into another room, and I was denied the chance to speak or understand what was happening. I felt a deep anger and frustration over my complete lack of control. On one hand, there was a flicker of hope—but it was quickly overshadowed by uncertainty. Two hours later, waited in the cell of the magistrate court, I was asked to board a minibus with other detainees, and the driver took us to San Vicente men's prison that day.

CHAPTER SIX

2 years

After I was taken into the men's prison, further away into the I was escorted by army soldiers and handed over to the prison' guards. They took me to the Director's office, and I was asked to sign in for my incarceration there. After, I signed, I was escorted into the cells by the prison guards. While I was escorted inside, I saw detainees looking out through the long cells bars dividing the main entrance to the open area and dormitories cells, and then, they saw me, and they started asking me, "are you a common or political?". I responded "political". They told me that there was a group inside of political prisoners and I could go to them, but it was late that day and the guards took me to one of the cell dormitories, I did not know anyone, and I asked the guard where I can sleep that night, and he replied "you can sleep under a bunkbed on the floor". One hour later, I heard a guard's voice over the loud prison' speaker, directing all detainees, that it was time to enter their dormitories cells, and after the prison guards locked each that evening. I did not have nothing to eat that night, as I was not hungry, and I only have a piece of cloth with me to keep me warm the first night of my illegal imprisonment at the men's prison.

The next day, I woke up by the prison's speakers guard' voice, which directed all detainees "it was time to get out the dormitories cells". I went outside, and I started looking for the political detainees, and I found the group, I introduced myself and I told them who I was an illegally detained by the Guardia National and I was sent to the prison for no valid reason, they all welcomed me to the group, and they invited me to stay with them during the day to eat and hang out with them. I learned that all the detainees of the political group, were members of other NGO's like me, and they got arrested, torture and detained like me, they supported me throughout the two years of imprisonment in the prison, I eat with them, an got medicine when I was unwell and gave emotional support.

A year has passed of my imprisonment, when a raid took place. I was afraid and scare to death. I vividly remembered that it was a sunny day, just before lunch, when I heard a gun shoot fired by one of the prison guards who started yelling at a detainee who was trying to escape that day. He was climbing the roof of one of the dormitories cells, when another prison guard shoot him twice, but he missed. More gunshots were shot at, and all detainees started to run towards the dormitories' cells for cover. I was seated with a friend, I met a couple months ago, he was seated in front of me, and we were enjoying a cuppa of coffee, when I heard a bullet penetrating something soft, then, I realised that the bullet hit his back of his head and come through his left eye and he eye socker started to bleed. My reflect was to crutch and fall on my back with my hands over my head. His blood stein my left shoe, immediately, and I stood up and started running to the dormitory cell, that it was in front of me for cover. Hours passed by and I could hear detainees' screaming *"stop killing us your busters"*. And more shoots were discharged. It became late and dark, no one that night was in their dormitories' cells, as prison guards never came down from their post at the roof tops around the prison. That night was the longest night I have ever had, there was no light, electricity cut down, no food served. I could sense that fear was in the air and detainee's anger was manifested by anger, looting and fires were let in the prison, a complete loss of control for the attempt scape of a detainee and the death of one of the detainees that day.

A few weeks went by, and I found that there was not an investigation for the death of the person I was having coffee with during the raids. I assumed the Director's prison was not going to call for media conference and report what has happened at the prison to the community, and he never did. I felt disappointed and I realised impunity is everywhere, including in prison systems. Once again, I felt powerless for impunity of the death in custody, by prison guards who were responsible and never took responsibility for their actions. I reluctantly decided to let go, and I focused on continued learning playing my guitar and wood carving. One day, I recorded my voice over a Bukis cassette and sent it to the women's prison. I later learned that it had finally been received—only after the prison director listened to it herself. Eventually, I was granted permission to make a 30-minute phone call once a month, from the men's director's office to the women's director's office. This small connection helped me feel a sense of contact and hope.

After a year of being illegally imprisonment, I managed to complete my year 9. This was a good achievement for me as I did not let the system to break my spirit, as my resilience grown as I longer I was in the prison. I started to read books, learning to play the guitar and wood carving flowers. I focused on leaning new skills and graduate for my year 9, as I never was able to do when I was out of prison, as I needed to work to provide for myself. I started to accept that I may stayed longer at the prison and my strategy was to keep my mind busy to learn things I never have the opportunity to. I managed to change the purpose of my illegal imprisonment to a leaning opportunity. I had ongoing communication and updates from our lawyers and after 2 years they finally had news for us.

Our lawyers told us that I needed to attend the jury in San Salvador and the prison guards will take me. The day of the hearing came, and I was taken to the magistrate hearing that day. I remembered the prosecutor of government alleged that we were communists, a danger to society, we had blown up homemade bombs to destroy public electricity supplies and to create fear in San Salvador, and then our lawyers argued against the prosecutors that we were not what they said we were and were fabricated lies. After one hours of the hearing the jury went to private room to decide for us our freedom. The jury was not convinced, as there was no evidence of the alleged and unfounded lies against me, as members of NGO's in the city. In 1980 and 90s In El Salvador, all members of a NGO's were persecuted, killed, illegally imprisoned or reported missing. Sometimes wonder why were able to be spare by the Guardian National as we knew that they have arrested other co-workers prior to us and were illegally arrested and later detained.

I was released after the jury dropped the case, ruling that there was no evidence of any wrongdoing on my part. Our case was the very first case gone to a jury in the legal El Salvador's legal system.

I were illegally detained for 2 years in separate prisons, she was incarcerated into women's prison near San Salvador. I was incarcerated further away in one of the central prisons of the country, so far that only whose who were willing to visit me did, but no one did. Except for members of the International Red Cross who would visit the prison for political prisoners' welfare checks, like me and the others in the prison. The distance was part of punishment for those incarcerated in the prison, as considered political prisoners at that time by the Salvadoran backed US government.

CHAPTER SEVEN

The role of the media

I remembered that our families were afraid to visit us, one of the reasons was the media. Back in the 80s and 90s he media in El Salvador seemed to bias and sided on the government. I experienced media bias to a personal level. A week after my illegal imprisonment, I discovered that my photograph had been featured on the front page of two major newspapers in El Salvador. I found out when a detainee's family visited the prison over the weekend and brought one of the papers. I recognized my own face and the future mother of my children on the cover of the newspapers and asked if I could read it—they agreed. The cover page of the newspaper had two photographs of me side by side and it read "*NGOs =FMLN*". The newspaper was accusing us of being members of the FMLN a revolutionary organisation, and we were working undercover with the NGOs to taught communist to the communities that we were helping in San Salvador. The accusations against us by the newspaper were totally fabricated and unfounded lies. Before, I was arbitrated arrested and illegally imprisonment, I have had an idea how media could be used "fake news" to convince people that my I was a communist, but then I realeased how much power the media had at that time, and how bias they were to side with the Salvadorian government's culture of fear. The newspaper had already made us guilty without due process. They intentions seemed to me was to use our illegal detention and imprisonment, to justice the military's arbitrated persecution to NGOs in El Salvador by linked our NGOs to the FMLN a revolutionary organisation. The newspaper also intended to character assassination by stated that we were communists a word that I was not familiar with till the newspaper mentioned it in their cover page at that time.

The newspaper seemed to have taken a decision, for themselves, of their one-sided view without any due process of defamation against us. They not only contributed to the persecution of my colleagues after their lies but also to other NGOs in San Salvador.

After the media coverage of our case, our arrest and illegal imprisonment news went "viral". It is interesting that before contemporary social media like TikTok to mentioned some, the newspapers of El Salvador during the 80s thru the 90s, were in the business of generate "fake news", to discredited people working in NGOs and normalised persecution, oppression and violence against civilians in our society. The media seemed to normalised victimisation, torture and culture of death during the period of civil war in El Salvador. The media controlled the narrative of what was normal and socially acceptable in everyday life in our country. Morning newspapers covers promoted division, suspicious and fear, which undermined our democracy values of our civil society and human rights, particularly members of society that were critical of the El Salvador's government of the day for its oppressive policies and breaches of human rights.

CHAPTER EIGHT

Internal refugee communities

*E*merging of temporary internal refugees' family's communities on public land and parks in the city of San Salvador become a reality during the period of 80s and 90s. These emerging marginalised communities were peasant's families' survivors of trauma after fleeing their homes, land and livelihoods due to the indiscriminatory bombardment of the air military forces with the excuse that they were communists. Families fleet to the city of San Salvador for safety and they started to build their homes in unoccupied lands with cardboard and anything they could use to housed themselves and their families. They faced many issues including lack of access to basic needs like drinking water, health services, electricity, sanitation, employment. Once again, when these communities started to emerge, the Media started to demonised them by published photographs of the communities in their newspaper covers labelled them as illegal thieves of public spaces, with disregards to local councils' rules and regulation of land ownership, and public nuisance. The government never acknowledged the reason for the emerging communities in the city, nor the media newspapers of bombardment of their homes and for that reason internal refugees families to flee and moved to the city for safety. The communities started to experienced oppression and discrimination by the local councils, by issued eviction orders to relocate somewhere else. Our NGOs emerged as a community organisation to advocate and give a voice to homeless people after the earthquake on 10 of October 1986 in El Salvador. As member of the NGOs my co-workers and I, visited these communities to offer support and conducted research on their basis needs, mental health and wellbeing. Community engagement opportunities of these marginalised and concentrated poverty communities of internal refugees' families by government never took place. The displacement of these internal refugees' families was the outcome of the military indiscriminatory bombardment into their homes in rural El Salvador. Our NGOs was the only community organisation that was interested not only to assist these communities with basis needs but also with community development initiatives and advocacy to addressing their communities' needs. My co-workers and I conducted regular visits to the communities to collect data on number of children, pregnant women and the elderly. We identified needs, and started to address them with limited sources that our NGOs could provided to them including, immunisation, food humpers, and setting up public septic bathrooms with the help of members.

Government engagement with NGOs never happens nor they were interest to work with us, they were more preoccupied to wanting to know where our resources came from, who were the donors, and how our organising received them. The military spent their resources and technology to spy on our organisation, to find "something wrong", instead of working in partnership with us as NGOs organisation not only to provide basis needs to internal refugee families' communities who were marginalised and discriminated against by the Media newspapers. Our NGOs saw potential in each member of those communities, and I hoped the government did by making investments in grassroots community initiatives to provide training and education for young men to gained skills and be employable to provide for their families and hopefully be able to have their homes and live a safe and happier lives with dignity.

CHAPTER NINE

Time to leave

I am seating down in my chair, in one of the counselling rooms at work, it's 1pm, Friday's afternoon, I had "a day of cancellations", as session after session were cancelled, I am certain that the cancellations were not reflecting on me as "counsellor". Then, I continue seen in front of me, a 4-section glass window, and the trees outside, with their branches fully blooming with small, but, full foliage of write flowers in each branch, swinging gently, side by side by the afternoon's breeze, as a reminder, it's spring in full swing. It is October in Canberra. As I am here seating in front of my desk and typing this words that coming out of mind. I started to remembered the time I knew we needed to leave El Salvador.

After I was finally released from two years of illegal imprisonment. We stayed with family and friend, but we just could not adjust to back to normal lives after how we have been treated by the government and its legal system. I remembered that one of aunties told that her ex-husband applied for visa to migrate to Australia, and we went to visited her to ask for more information. She was happy to see me, knowing what I had been through. She invited me to lunch and shared information about the Australian Consulate in San Salvador. The next day we went to the address where the Consulate was located, that my auntie gave us. When we arrived we saw a sliding meal gate with only a number but did have nothing else to identify the building as consulate, we decided to knot the metal gate and soon after a person came out and she asked, *"you how can I help you?"*. We told her that we were told that the place is the Australian Consulate in San Salvador, the person responded, ye it is. We felt a sense of relief and we then told the person in we could see someone to talk about our case to migrate. The person asked to follow her and a few moments after she introduced us to the Consulate in the office, she greeted us and asked to take a seat, and we sat down. The Consulate asked us how she could help us and then we told her our history and reason we wanted to flee the country as we no longer felt safe. The Consulate gave a form to complete and told us that we have two weeks to bring all required documents and including the form she gave us. At that time, we both were working and manage to find time to get all the required documents to the Consulate with our application. The required documents included an affidavit by an organisation that could proof that we were in prison as political prisoners. I remembered that staff from the Red Cross used to visit the men's prison to do welfare check and health checks for political prisoners. I needed to go to the Red Cross HQ office in San Salvador to help us. The following week we found time to visit the Red Cross HQ and we went and when we arrived, we introduced ourselves and requesting to speak with the person who can help us with the affidavit. We were told that the manager was away that day, but she would back to the office the following day. We went back home that afternoon and wrapped up for the day. The following day we prepared to meet with the Red Cross manager, and he was there at the office when we arrived. We introduced ourselves and asked if he could help us with our application by writing an affidavit confirming that staff from the Red Cross visited us while we were imprisonment. He was supportive and wrote the affidavit and gave to it to us.

The next day we went back to the Consulate and hand out our application with the affidavit to the Consular, she said to us that we need to wait for 5 days for our application to be assessed. We thanked the Consular for her help and then we went back to work for the rest of the day. My sleep issues continued and were getting worse as I had nightmares every night since we were released from prison. My family used to give paracetamol to help me, but it helped only for a while. My nightmares were when we were tortured by the military in the barracks for the 3 days, they arbitrary arrested us for no reason and I would woke up screaming and sweat. After 5 days we returned to the Consulate office to find out the outcome of our application to migrate. We went into the office and asked for the Consular and they took us to her office. We waited a few minutes in her office and then she came and told us that she has good news. She invited us to sat down and started to told us the process going forward with the migration visas for us.

I am grateful to the International Red Cross in San Salvador for assisting me with my refugee application. They provided a written affidavit after visiting me during my illegal imprisonment. Their Affidavit was sufficient evidence for our application to leave the country as we lived in fear at that time. The members of the consulate helped us with everything we needed to flee including, organising our Permanent Visas for resettlement to Australia, flights to flown from El Salvador, to Los Angeles, and to Sydney and finally, to Albury/Wodonga. I always grateful for the Australian' consulate in San Salvador for helping us to flee El Salvador in 1990's to resettle to Australia. I am thankful for their act of kindness by helping us for a new start in our lives and to resettled in our new adopted mother land, Australia.

Migrating to Australia with my family gave us a strong sense of hope and excitement for new beginnings and a fresh start in our adopted homeland, Down Under. Australia an ancient continent where, climate, culture flora and fauna are so different to El Salvador, where I was born, instead of having coffee farms, cotton and cane of sugar fields, but here, we have mostly eucalyptus and wattles trees, and of course if drive to the north Queensland is a bit similar landscape or depending on where you live in Australia.

CHAPTER TEN

Current situation

I have been reflecting on how El Salvador has been changing for the last few years with under the new President, Nayid Bukele. I have noticed through the media what has been happening in El Salvador. I can see that El Salvador is finally, going through a significant positive social and economic development changes. The country has started to be transformed into a symbol of hope for others in Las Americas. Las *"Maras"*, gangs seemed to be a nightmare of the past.

Before the current changes in El Salvador, I like to share with you the reader, the history of my oldest niece., Johana. She was only 5 years old last time I saw her; she was a child, and I remembered that I sent her, three years after I migrated to Australia, a soft doll for her to play. It was difficult to keep in touch with my sister due to the distance and limiting means of communication at that time. But my sister and my niece always were in my prayers. A few years later I found out that my sister married, and she started a new family and life with her new husband. Years passed by and they have 4 children, 3 sons and one daughter but my niece moved out as she wanted to start living in her own. She was a good student, and she was working part time in catering. But one day, my sister message me thought fakebook's messenger and told the sad news about my niece.

My oldest niece was one of the tens of thousands of young women that were killed by gangs' criminals in 2000 in San Salvador. I remembered that day when my sister messaged me thru Facebook's messager. to tell the saddest news, I was shocked and heartbroken. My sister told me that the only reason to explained why my niece was killed by gangs, was because, she refused to be dating one of them, and her refusal cost her life. A day after she went missing on her way back home, her mutilated naked body was found on the streets. She was on her way home after work when she went missing and never made it home. After the death of my oldest niece, my sister told me that she and her four teenage sons and daughter were no longer felt safe and always on guard. She requested to help her, get out the country, as she no longer felt safe for her and her four teenagers. I tried by reached people I knew in local Government, but I was told that it was up the federal government to help, and after a few weeks of calls and asking for a meeting my request for helping my sister and her 4 teenagers went into deft hears. Fortunately, my sister and my mother in New York, US were able to help them to migrate to US under the triangle Permanent Visa for refugees from El Salvador, Guatemala and Honduras. These countries were classified by the UN a triangle of high risk of homicide mostly for women spacing homicide gender violence. I was relief and happy that my sister could helped them in time of crisis to leave El Salvador and migrate to US to have a new start in their life and safe. After all these years of living in the US, I kept in connected with my sister, she shared with me, their everyday lives with my nephews and niece, work and feeling safer living now in New York. I glad that they're safer. Then, one of my family member asked, "Are you okay? You looked like you disappeared into your thoughts." I responded, "No, I'm here with you." Rocío's show ended, and we went to bed that night. As I lay down in bed, staring up at the bedroom ceiling, I heard the wind whisper outside. *"A windy night,"* I said quietly. A family member suggested, *"Yes, let's try to get some sleep."* I replied, *"Yes, let's try. Thank you for today."* Then, I reflected on what I was grateful for—everything I had done that day. I thought, *"I'm grateful to be home, safe under this roof with my family."* And then I fell asleep.

The emerging and establishment of Las Maras, La Salvachucha and Barrio 18, in El Salvador, it is important to look back where they originated. According to the Roy, 2022, the Maras, MS-13 and its main rival Barrio 18 were transnational criminal organizations that originated in the United States. Both were founded in Los Angeles in the 1980s by Salvadoran refugees who fled the country's civil war pursuing the so called, *"The American Dream"*. Same of these Salvadoran refugees were involved and committed crimes and therefore they were incarcerated. During this time the then U.S. President Bill Clinton, signed a series of laws expanding the scope of deportable offenses, tens of thousands of Salvadorans were expelled, and their gang without officially notifying the Salvadoran government of their deportations, and then they developed networks flourished back home in the postwar chaos. He further argues that gang violence remains at the center of the region's migration crisis, which has intensified since 2014. The consequences of gang violence contributed to triggered a mass migration of Salvadorean to US border looking for safety and opportunities for a better life. By 2019, Salvadorans made up 37 percent of all Central American migrants at the southern U.S. border. "

The gangs and their imprisonment.

From a historical perspective, Las Mara members, were Salvadorian refugees who migrated to US with the hope to find so called, *"the American*

Dream". Some of them were involved in gang violence and crime and ended up incarcerated. The former president, Maurio Funes brokered a controversial truce with gangs, Mara Salvachucha and El Barrio 18, in El Salvador in 2012, but it felt apart in 2014 and by 2015 El Salvador was considered the deadliest country in the Western Atmosphere with 105 homicides for 100,000 people5.

El Salvador's Homicide Rate Plummeted After 2015

Homicides per 100,000 people

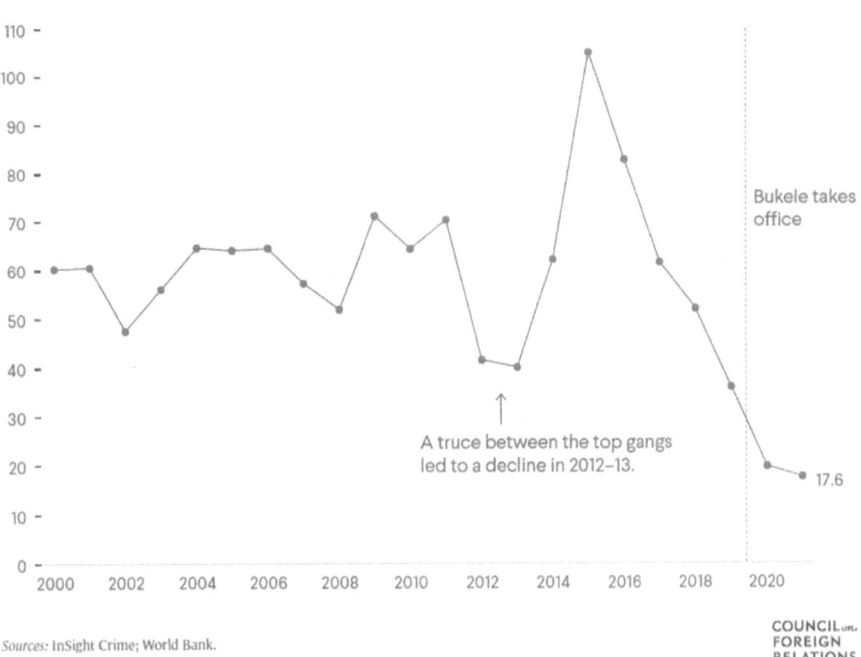

Bukele takes office

A truce between the top gangs led to a decline in 2012–13.

17.6

Sources: InSight Crime; World Bank.

COUNCIL on FOREIGN RELATIONS

In El Salvador, a new mega jail was built in 2022, by the Salvadoran government with the objective to imprison gangs' members who are considered *"high ranking criminals"*. The prison is named CECOT (Centre for the Confinement of Terrorism), (Ventas7, 2024). The mega prison represents the commitment of El Salvadorean Government of elected president Nayid Bukele's to safeguard the Salvadorean society against from gangs' violence, making now the country the safer in the Western Atmosphere compared to 2015, when homicides by gang violence were the higher in the Americas. A shift

Image: Government of El Salvador

Cecot is located in Tecoluca, 74km (46 miles) south-east of the capital, San Salvador

Source *https://www.bbc.com/news/world-latin-america-68244963*

CONCLUSION

*G*ang violence not only contributed to keep in El Salvador as the most violent country in the Western Atmosphere during the twenty century, but also to the high number of Salvadorans' mass migration compare to other central American countries, to the south border of US in history. Salvadoreans did not only loss their homes and livelihoods due to gang violence, but also, they seemed to be prepared to leave everything behind with the hope to find safety and new start in their lives abroad. This reality of flee El Salvador for safety was the reason for my family and I that we decided to migrate to Australia under the refugee settlement program of the UN. I knew that to migrate through Guatemala and Mexico to south border of the US, we could never make it, but we were most certain that we wanted to migrate and live in a country far away from US.

In El Salvador during the 80s through the 90s the Salvadorian government's ideology and policies considered "communists" those who helped and advocated for the oppressed and marginalised and were community orientated. and therefore, you were a problem to be eradicated. I remembered, that at that time, the Salvadorean government was not willing nor be open, to work in collaboration or consultation engagement with the NGOs sector. As a NGOs our organisation, worked with and assisted, marginalised members of communities with grassroots community development initiatives conducive to educate its community stakeholders to learn basis medical skills including immunisation, to vaccinate their own children's, pregnant women and the elderly to preventable diseases to mentioned some. The purpose of NGOs work was to enable communities, not only to have their basis needs met, but also to develop their own capability to have access to education and self-employment to provide for themselves. I don't think this is communist, but rather altruistic and humanistic values by helping others in need as my grandmother taught me.

The Guardia Nacional, a military section of the Salvadoran army, tortured me, and the media in the '90s labeled me as a communist. These were significant factors in my decision to migrate to Australia, seeking safety and a new life where my children could grow up free from oppression, torture, and trauma. I always grateful for the opportunity to be allowed to be resettled in Australia. We have been able to be raised three smart, responsible and community minded adults, they have given us three beautiful grandchildren that I cherished every day. I hope that one day my family and I are not only to be confident and comfortable to visit El Salvador but also to be emotionally ready to do so. I still have a lot of scars in my heart to heal. Though, I feel humble and proud on how El Salvador starts to be a place to travel and visit, thanks for the efforts of the current elected president, Nayid Bukele's policies and his government to keep the country safer where Salvadoreans live and enjoy life where todo azul again.

REFERENCE

1. National Institute of Mental Health. (2022). Helping Children and Adolescents Cope With Traumatic Events (NIH Publication No. 22-MH-8066). U.S. Department of Health and Human Services, National Institutes of Health. Retrieved January 11, 2023, from https://www.nimh.nih.gov/sites/default/files/documents/health/ publications/helping-children-and-adolescents-cope-with-disasters-and-other-traumatic-events/helping-children-and-adolescents-cope-with-traumatic-events.pdf

2. Avery, B. (2020, January 21). PTSD Recovery and Overcoming Fear, HealthyPlace. Retrieved on 2024, October 20 from https://www.healthyplace.com/blogs/traumaptsdblog/2020/1/ ptsd-recovery-and-overcoming-fear

3. D H Harlow, David H. W A, Randall A. R, Michael J. A G., Salvador (1993) The San Salvador earthquake of 10 October 1986 and its historical context. https://ui.adsabs.harvard.edu/ abs/1993BuSSA..83.1143H/abstract#:~:text=The%20San%20 Salvador%20earthquake%20of%2010%20October%201986%20 resulted%20in,(M6%E2%88%92)%20of%205.74

4. Gibb, T (2000) The Guardian newspaper
    https://www.theguardian.com/theguardian/2000/mar/23/
    features11.g21

5. Roy, D. (2022) Why gangs violence spiked in El Salvador.
    https://www.cfr.org/in-brief/why-has-gang-violence-spiked-el-
    salvador-bukele#:~:text=President%20Mauricio%20Funes%20
    took%20a,105%20homicides%20per%20100%2C000%20people.

6. Wells, M (2013) El Salvador Spent in Security no Social Welfare
    World Bank.
    https://insightcrime.org/news/brief/el-salvador-has-low-public-
    spending-concentrated-in-security-world-bank/

7. Ventas, L (2024) Coming face to face with inmates in El Salvador's
    mega-jail. BBC World news.
    https://www.bbc.com/news/world-latin-america-68244963